Who Was
George Washington
Carver?

Who Was George Washington Carver?

By Jim Gigliotti

Illustrated by Stephen Marchesi

Grosset & Dunlap
An Imprint of Penguin Random House

For Dante and Sophia, that you might always keep your
passion for learning—JG

GROSSET & DUNLAP
Penguin Young Readers Group
An Imprint of Penguin Random House LLC

Library of Congress Cataloging-in-Publication Data is available.

ISBN 978-0-448-48312-2   10 9 8 7 6 5 4 3 2 1

Contents

Who Was
George Washington Carver?

Mrs. Baynham looked out at her garden, but she didn't like what she saw. Mrs. Baynham lived in the biggest house in Diamond Grove, Missouri, in the mid-1870s. Inside the house, everything was in order: pretty paintings and nice furniture. But outside, in the garden, her roses weren't blooming.

Why not? she wondered. Her friend Susan Carver's roses were blooming. Her roses were big and beautiful—and bright red! Mrs. Carver lived on a nearby farm. Mrs. Baynham went over and asked what her secret was to growing such perfect flowers.

"It's our George," Mrs. Carver said. "He's the one who knows about roses."

George was the ten-year-old boy who lived with Mrs. Carver. She was his foster mother. Mrs. Carver had been taking care of George since he was a baby. And George had been taking care of Mrs. Carver's plants and flowers.

Actually, George helped out around the farm in many ways. He loved Mrs. Carver as if she were his own mother. He would have done just about anything she asked. But he was especially happy when she asked him to help with her garden.

So George went over to Mrs. Baynham's house to take a look at her roses. He knew right away what was wrong.

Her roses needed to be moved to a different part of the garden, where they could get more sun. He moved the plants, and soon they were in full bloom!

Word spread quickly. And young George started helping many of Mrs. Carver's friends with their plants and flowers. One week, a neighbor needed help with her lilies. Another week, a friend asked for help with her begonias. George always seemed to know how to  fix whatever problem there was. Soon, he became known as "the Plant Doctor."

George never lost that helpful spirit, nor his love for plants and the best way to grow them. He was George Washington Carver, and he used his passion for nature to become one of the most famous, and helpful, scientists in the world.

Chapter 1
Orphaned

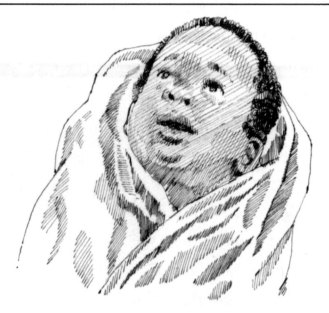

George Washington Carver was born into slavery in Diamond Grove, Missouri, near the end of the American Civil War, which was fought from 1861 to 1865. George was black; his owners, Moses and Susan Carver, were white.

Moses and Susan were German immigrants. They didn't like slavery, but they had a 240-acre farm that needed much work, and Missouri had entered the Union in 1820 as a slave state. In 1855, the Carvers purchased a thirteen-year-old slave girl named Mary. They treated Mary well and were happy for her when she gave birth to a son named Jim in 1859. Several years later, George was born.

No one knows exactly when George was born, because most records among slave owners were poorly kept. Most likely George was born in 1864. His father, Giles, was a slave who was owned by a neighbor of the Carvers. He was killed in a farming accident not long after George's birth. No one knows exactly how many brothers or sisters George had.

George lived with Mary and Jim in a small cabin on the Carver farm. The cabin was the original house on the farm. Moses and Susan had since built a larger house, and they lived in that one.

One night when George was still an infant, he was asleep in the cabin. Suddenly, there was the sound of men on horseback. Moses knew what that meant. Twice before, his farm had been attacked by raiders —called bushwhackers—who were fighting on the Confederate (Southern) side in the Civil War.

TERRITORIES

DISPUTED AREAS

UNION (FREE)

CONFEDERATE (SLAVE)

Missouri's role in the Civil War was complicated. Even though Missouri was a slave state, many of the people who lived there were against slavery. So some men on the Union (Northern) side fought for Missouri to remain as one of the United States and to free the slaves. But some of Missouri's men fought to create a separate nation that would keep slavery legal. They were on the Confederate side.

Moses was caught in the middle. He had slaves, but since he also wanted slavery to be illegal, he upset people on both sides.

The bushwhackers wanted to take the slaves and sell them in a nearby state such as Arkansas. Moses raced to the cabin and called out for Mary. Moses grabbed Jim, and Mary grabbed George.

Moses and Jim escaped, but it was too late for Mary and George. The men grabbed her and her baby, and they galloped away into the night.

The next day, Moses hurried to Neosho, Missouri, which was about eight miles away. There was a man in Neosho who was a scout for the Union side. The man might know where to look for Mary and George.

Several days later, the scout came back. He was clutching George, who was very sick with whooping cough, but alive. There was no sign of Mary. The raiders had abandoned George. Mary was never heard from again.

Jim and George were left without a father or a mother, but Moses and Susan were determined to give the boys a family. The Carvers moved Jim and George into the main house and treated them as if they were their own children.

Even though the Thirteenth Amendment freed all slaves in 1865, the boys stayed with the Carvers, whom they called "Uncle Moses" and "Aunt Susan." George was known simply as "Carver's George."

THE END OF SLAVERY

    PRESIDENT ABRAHAM LINCOLN'S EMANCIPATION PROCLAMATION WAS A BIG MOMENT IN US HISTORY. THE PROCLAMATION WAS ISSUED ON JANUARY 1, 1863. IT DECLARED THAT THE SLAVES IN THE TEN STATES FIGHTING ON THE CONFEDERATE (SOUTHERN) SIDE IN THE CIVIL WAR WERE FREE.

    TECHNICALLY, THE EMANCIPATION PROCLAMATION

HAD LITTLE EFFECT. THE CONFEDERATE STATES HAD TRIED TO LEAVE THE UNION AND WEREN'T ABOUT TO HONOR ANYTHING LINCOLN SAID. BUT IT WAS VERY IMPORTANT BECAUSE IT MADE CLEAR THAT THE CIVIL WAR WASN'T JUST ABOUT SAVING THE UNION, BUT ALSO WAS ABOUT ENDING SLAVERY.

WHEN THE UNION (NORTHERN) SIDE WON THE WAR, SLAVERY WAS OVER EVERYWHERE IN THE UNITED STATES. IT BECAME OFFICIAL WHEN THE THIRTEENTH AMENDMENT TO THE US CONSTITUTION TOOK EFFECT ON DECEMBER 6, 1865.

Chapter 2
Childhood

Every day, George explored the fields and flowers and animals on the Carver farm. It was a big farm, about the size of 180 football fields! Moses and Susan grew corn, wheat, and potatoes. They raised cows, pigs, and horses.

There was always plenty of work to do on the farm. Jim and George were expected to help the other farmhands as much as they could. Jim was big and did some of the chores that took strength, such as plowing the fields. But George never seemed to be fully healthy after he recovered from whooping cough as a baby. He was often sick.

ody was very feeble, and it was a constant
are between life and death to see who would
in the mastery," he once wrote.

Because he was often sick, and not very strong,

George was excused from the heavy-duty work on the farm. But he still wanted to be helpful. So he did what he could, such as taking care of the plants and flowers and feeding the animals.

George didn't go to school as a youngster, but he still had quite an education on the farm. From Moses, he learned to waste nothing. Moses believed that everything the family needed to live was available right there on the farm. From Susan, George learned how to sew, cook, and clean.

Susan even made her own clothes with the help of a spinning wheel she kept in the house.

When George was eight years old, he was baptized a Christian. Because he loved nature so much, George always referred to God as "Creator." George went to church on Sundays, about a mile away from the farm. During the week, he played with the neighborhood kids. Most of them were white, and he learned to get along with people no matter what color they were.

Mrs. Baynham was white. One day when George was helping her with her roses, she showed him the paintings in her house. George decided he wanted to paint pictures like that. He didn't have any brushes or paint or canvas or paper. But Moses had taught him to make good use of whatever was available. So George squeezed the juice out of some berries, took a small stick, and started painting on a flat rock.

When George wasn't working or playing,
he took long walks in the fields and the woods,
talking to plants and flowers, and caring for them.

He cleared a spot in the woods where he kept his own little nursery—a special place for plants. "Strange to say, all sorts of vegetation [plant life] seemed to thrive under my touch," he said.

He collected rocks, too, and stashed them by the chimney in a corner of the house. Susan would make him clean out the corner, but the pile would soon grow again.

George was incredibly curious. He wanted to learn everything he could about the plants and flowers and animals he saw every day. When he saw a coneflower, he wanted to know why it was purple. When he saw a black-eyed Susan, he wanted to know how it got its name.

Sometimes, Moses and Susan knew the answers—but not always. The Carvers had an old spelling book. George read the book cover to cover, but it didn't have the answers he was looking for, either. George wanted to go to school and learn all that he could.

Diamond Grove's school was in the same building where George went for church on Sundays. One day, he and Jim walked to the school. Imagine George's excitement at finally being able to find the answers to all of his questions! And imagine his disappointment at being told that the school was for white children only.

The kids George went to church with on Sundays and played with in the neighborhood could go to school, but he and Jim couldn't. They walked back home.

Jim went right back to helping out on the farm, but that wasn't enough for George. He didn't give up his dream of going to school.

When he was about thirteen, George went to Moses and Susan and told them he wanted to leave. They were the only parents he had ever known, and he loved them very much, but he wanted to go to school. His plan was to hike to Neosho, which had the nearest school for black children.

Moses and Susan always said the boys were free, and they could leave if they wished, so they didn't stop George. The next day, Susan packed up some snacks for George, and he began the long walk to Neosho.

By the time George made it to Neosho, the snacks were long gone. It was getting dark fast. George didn't know anybody in the town, and he didn't have any money. He was tired, and he was hungry.

George spotted a barn. He'd grown up on a farm, so a barn was a friendly place. There was no one inside. He set down his belongings, and soon was fast asleep.

Chapter 3
School Days

When George woke up the next morning, he stepped outside. The owner of the barn, Mariah Watkins, saw him. She figured he was hungry, so she fixed him some breakfast in the main house.

"What's your name?" Mariah asked him.

"I'm Carver's George," he said.

That sounded as if Carver owned George.
Mrs. Watkins, who was black, didn't like that.
Slavery had ended more than ten years earlier,
and nobody owned anyone else. So Mrs. Watkins
called him "George Carver."

George told Mrs. Watkins that he was in
Neosho to go to school. He didn't have a place to
live yet, but he'd figure something out.

Mrs. Watkins was a kind woman, so she told George he could stay with her and her husband, Andrew. But she also was a strict, no-nonsense woman. If George was going to live there and go to the nearby Lincoln School—named after Abraham Lincoln—he'd have to do his share of the chores. George was delighted with that deal. He already could clean house and do laundry.

Moses Carver had taught George not to waste anything. Now Mrs. Watkins taught him not to waste any time. She expected him to go to school during the day, but to come home at recess and do laundry. After school, he would clean the house and maybe help cook dinner.

George and Mr. and Mrs. Watkins read the Bible during the week, and they went to church on Sundays. Sometimes, George walked back to Diamond Grove to visit Moses and Susan and Jim on the weekends.

Neosho was different than Diamond Grove.

There were about 3,300 people living there—
almost three times as many people as in Diamond
Grove. And about one of every eight residents
in Neosho was black. Diamond Grove had only
sixteen black people living in the whole town
when George grew up there.

George stayed in Neosho for a year or so, and learned just about all he could at the one-room Lincoln School. "This simply sharpened my appetite for more knowledge," he wrote. He found that if he wanted more schooling, he'd have to move again . . . and again . . . and again.

At the time, many former slaves were moving from the South into Kansas and other Northern states in search of a better life. In 1878, George hitched a ride with one such family on the way to Fort Scott, Kansas. George rode in the back of a wagon for part of the eighty-mile trip and walked the rest of the way.

In 1879, he moved to Olathe, Kansas. In 1880, he moved to Minneapolis, Kansas, and then to Paola, Kansas.

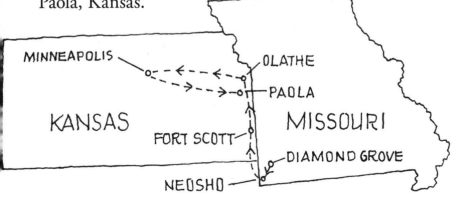

MINNEAPOLIS

OLATHE

PAOLA

KANSAS

MISSOURI

FORT SCOTT

DIAMOND GROVE

NEOSHO

At each stop, George's agreeable personality and willingness to work hard made it easy for him to find a family to take him in. In Fort Scott, he moved in with Felix and Mattie Payne and their family. Felix was a blacksmith. In Olathe, George moved in with C.C. and Lucy Seymour. George helped Mrs. Seymour with her laundry business. (In time, he moved with their family to Minneapolis.) In Paola, he moved in with Willis and Delilah Moore. These were all black families who lived in mostly white towns.

In this period, "sunshine and shadow were profusely intermingled," George wrote. In other words, there were both good times and bad times. The good times included finding schools in every town he lived. He never wanted to stop learning. One classmate remembered that George, who had grown to be six feet tall and thin, would rather collect plants and leaves at recess than play games.

The bad times, however, included cruel encounters with racism. The worst of it came in Fort Scott, where George witnessed a lynching—a black man being murdered by a group of white men. "As young as I was, the horror haunted me," he said. George left Fort Scott shortly after.

Other instances involved George personally. In one town, he and a white friend went out to breakfast. When they sat down, the waiter told them he would serve the white man, but not George. This kind of racism was legal in those days under "Jim Crow" laws.

In 1883, George got word that his brother, Jim, had died from smallpox. Jim was twenty-three years old. He had left the Carver farm a few years earlier and moved to Arkansas to find work. Although George had not seen his brother much after leaving home, he wrote that he felt "as never before that I was left alone."

JIM CROW LAWS

IN 1865, THE THIRTEENTH AMENDMENT OFFICIALLY ENDED SLAVERY. BUT BLACKS IN THE UNITED STATES, ESPECIALLY IN THE SOUTH, STILL SUFFERED UNDER JIM CROW LAWS. THE LAWS WERE NAMED AFTER AN OFFENSIVE BLACK CHARACTER FROM A SONG IN THE 1800S. THESE LAWS KEPT BLACKS FROM USING THE SAME RESTAURANTS AND HOTELS AS WHITES DID. AND THEY ALLOWED FOR "SEPARATE-BUT-EQUAL" FACILITIES, SUCH AS RESTROOMS OR DRINKING FOUNTAINS, FOR BLACKS AND WHITES. IN REALITY, WHILE FACILITIES WERE SEPARATE, THEY USUALLY WEREN'T EQUAL. PLACES RESERVED FOR BLACKS WERE OFTEN MUCH WORSE THAN THOSE FOR WHITES.

SOME JIM CROW LAWS LASTED UNTIL ONE HUNDRED YEARS AFTER THE END OF THE AMERICAN CIVIL WAR. IN 1954, THE US SUPREME COURT ENDED SEPARATE SCHOOLS FOR BLACKS AND WHITES. IN 1965, CIVIL-RIGHTS LAWS FINALLY PUT AN END TO "SEPARATE-BUT-EQUAL."

George found comfort, though, in friends who cared about him. He moved back in with the Seymour family in Minneapolis. This is where George took his middle name. When he began getting mail intended for a different George Carver in town, he added the initial *W* to his name so the postman could tell the two men apart. A friend asked if the *W* stood for Washington. George thought that sounded good, so he became known from then on as George Washington Carver.

George opened a laundry business—washing and drying clothes for other people—in Minneapolis, and bought a small plot of land.

Then he sold the land for a profit and moved to the larger town of Kansas City. He entered a school to learn shorthand and typewriting.

He thought he might want to work for a telegraph office. But he decided business school wasn't enough. George wanted to go to college. So he began writing to colleges he might attend.

Chapter 4
College Man

In 1884, an envelope addressed to George Washington Carver arrived from Highland College in Highland, Kansas. George ripped open the envelope. The school had accepted George as a student. He was going to college!

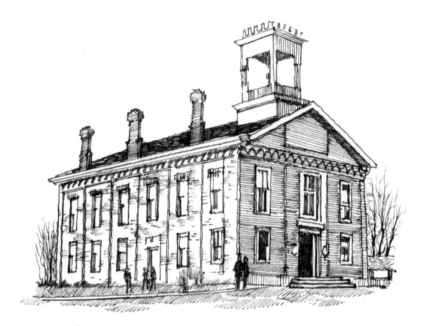

George was thrilled. He packed his bags, said good-bye to his friends, and took the train to Highland, about seventy-five miles away. But when he arrived on campus, school administrators told him he couldn't attend after all. He was black, and the school didn't accept nonwhites. Highland didn't know George was black when he applied by mail.

George was crushed. He was twenty years old, and he had no idea what to do next. He stayed in Highland about a year, cleaning and doing laundry for the Beeler family there. When the Beelers' son moved to Ness County, Kansas, in the mid-1880s to become a homesteader, George went with him. In Ness County, George worked for another settler named George Steeley, then claimed his own homestead.

Frontier life was difficult. In western Kansas, George built a small house made of sod.

Sod is made of pads of grass, its roots, and the dirt the roots are clinging to. The house was fourteen feet on each side. He kept it "neat, clean, and decorated with flowers and objects of interest," according to one neighbor. George planted vegetables and raised hens. Summers were hot, winters were cold, and water was sometimes hard to find. Communities of homesteaders were often close-knit groups regardless of color.

HOMESTEADING

WITH PLENTY OF LAND AVAILABLE FOR SETTLING ON THE US FRONTIER, PRESIDENT ABRAHAM LINCOLN SIGNED INTO LAW THE HOMESTEAD ACT OF 1862. IT ALLOWED SETTLERS, CALLED HOMESTEADERS, TO FILE A CLAIM FOR 160 ACRES OF PUBLIC LAND. THE HOMESTEADERS AGREED TO LIVE ON THE LAND, IMPROVE IT, AND FARM IT FOR FIVE YEARS. AT THE END OF FIVE YEARS, THEY HAD TO PAY ONLY A SMALL FEE—IT WAS $24 WHEN GEORGE WASHINGTON CARVER WAS A HOMESTEADER—TO BECOME THE LANDOWNERS. IF THEY DIDN'T WANT TO WAIT FIVE YEARS, HOMESTEADERS COULD PURCHASE THE LAND FOR $1.25 AN ACRE AFTER ONLY SIX MONTHS.

MOST HOMESTEADING TOOK PLACE IN THE LAND WEST OF THE MISSISSIPPI RIVER. MORE THAN 1.6 MILLION PEOPLE MADE HOMESTEAD CLAIMS. IT WAS AN OPPORTUNITY FOR FARMERS AND FREED SLAVES TO OWN THEIR OWN LAND AND TO BUILD BETTER LIVES FOR THEMSELVES.

BUT THE HOMESTEAD ACT WAS POSSIBLE ONLY BECAUSE THE US GOVERNMENT HAD FORCED SO MANY NATIVE AMERICANS OFF THEIR LAND.

George, one of the few black people in the area, was well-liked. He painted and sketched, played his accordion, and was helpful to neighbors. George planted trees and collected hundreds of plants. He watched carefully to see which plants grew best under what conditions.

Before his five years were up, George bought the homestead with the help of a bank loan.

But he couldn't make a living as a farmer. The soil was poor, and Kansas suffered a terrible drought. So in 1888, George moved to Iowa. Eventually, he turned over his homestead to the bank.

In Iowa, George lived in Winterset, a mostly white town where he found a job as a cook in a hotel. In church one Sunday, a woman in the choir named Helen Milholland noticed George. She enjoyed his high-pitched singing voice. The next day, she sent her husband, Dr. John Milholland, to talk to George at the hotel and to invite him to their home.

George made weekly visits to the Milholland home and attended church with them. They became great friends. The Milhollands soon discovered George's interest in art, and they encouraged him to go to college to study it.

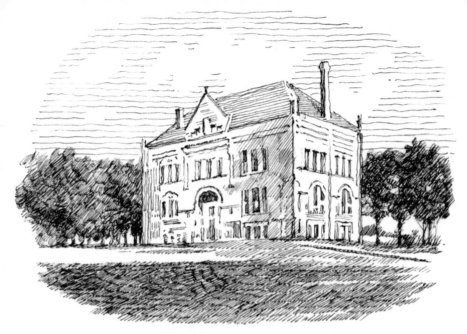

SIMPSON COLLEGE

There was a good school, called Simpson College, in nearby Indianola. George had been upset by the incident at Highland College and didn't want to go through that again. The Milhollands assured George that Simpson had no rule against blacks attending. They would even help with the application. So George applied, was accepted, and saved up his money for a year. He enrolled at Simpson in the fall of 1890.

George was only the second black student in the history of Simpson College, which had opened its doors thirty years earlier in 1860. He studied music and art, and he ran a laundry business to help pay tuition. But after he paid for his classes, he had almost nothing left over. "For quite one month I lived on prayer, beef suet [chunks of beef fat], and corn meal," he said, "and quite often without the suet and meal."

George was popular at Simpson with both his fellow students and his teachers. When they saw he was struggling to make ends meet, they snuck furniture, food, or other items into his room.

"They all seemed to take pride in seeing if he or she might not do more for me than someone else," George said.

In art class, sometimes George painted plants. Other times, he brought in his plants to show the teacher, Miss Budd. She was impressed with how much he knew about horticulture, the science of fruits, vegetables, and flowering plants.

She suggested that he consider attending Iowa State Agricultural School in Ames, Iowa. One reason was that her father taught science there. Another was that even though George was a very talented artist, she figured it would be difficult for anyone—especially a black man in the 1890s—to earn a living at it.

George knew Miss Budd was right. He also knew that even though his art might help bring people enjoyment, his knowledge of agriculture might help bring food to their dinner tables.

So after only one semester at Simpson, George enrolled at Iowa State in 1891. He studied chemistry, geology, botany, and zoology. In 1894, he became the first black person to graduate from Iowa State. When the school hired him as an assistant in botany (the science of plant life), George became the first black person to join the faculty there.

Chapter 5
The Greatest Good

George had no plans to leave Iowa State. He liked the faculty and the students there, and they liked him. He was studying for a graduate degree in agriculture and was teaching young men and women, too. It looked as if George was set for a long career at the school. But in April 1896, he received a letter that changed his life. It was from educator and orator Booker T. Washington.

Washington was perhaps the most famous black man in America in the late 1800s. In 1895, he gave a speech at the Cotton States and International Exposition in Atlanta, Georgia. The speech has come to be called the "Atlanta Compromise."

Washington essentially urged blacks to accept the idea of separate-but-equal in exchange for education, job training, and fairness in the court system. He wanted blacks to work with whites, not against them, to fight racism.

Not everyone agreed with Booker T. Washington. Some of his critics in the civil-rights movement felt that accepting separate-but-equal meant whites would always think blacks were not as good as they were. Booker T. Washington, of course, didn't believe that. But he believed that if blacks ever were to achieve true equality in the United States, they would need better education.

That was why Booker jumped at the chance to start an all-black school in Tuskegee, Alabama, in 1881. The Tuskegee Institute opened in a run-down, one-room building that year with just $2,000 from the state of Alabama. The next year, the school purchased one hundred acres of land, and the campus began to develop.

BOOKER T. WASHINGTON (1856–1915)

BOOKER TALIAFERRO WASHINGTON WAS BORN INTO SLAVERY. HE GREW UP TO BECOME AN EDUCATOR, AN AUTHOR, AND A WELL-KNOWN SPEAKER. IN 1881, HE ESTABLISHED THE TUSKEGEE INSTITUTE IN TUSKEGEE, ALABAMA, BECAUSE HE FELT THAT EDUCATION WAS THE BEST PATH FOR BLACK PEOPLE TO ACHIEVE TRUE EQUALITY.

IN HIS TIME, WASHINGTON WAS THE MOST FAMOUS LEADER OF THE BLACK COMMUNITY. IN 1901, HE BECAME THE FIRST BLACK PERSON TO BE OFFICIALLY INVITED TO THE WHITE HOUSE WHEN PRESIDENT THEODORE ROOSEVELT ASKED HIM TO DINNER.

THE TUSKEGEE INSTITUTE

Tuskegee wasn't a traditional college, like Iowa State, that accepted only high-school graduates. Instead, some Tuskegee students had as little as a fifth-grade education. Many of their parents and grandparents had been slaves. They were there for hands-on learning they could use in their day-to-day lives. As part of their classes, some early Tuskegee students actually built the classrooms that rose on the new campus.

Booker was still the president of the Tuskegee Institute when he wrote to George in 1896. The school was growing, Booker explained. He wanted to add a department of agriculture, and he wanted George to be in charge of it.

George had read about Booker's big Atlanta speech in the newspapers. George's beliefs about race relations were much the same as Booker's. George had lived among and worked with whites all his life. He believed that working with whites was the best path to equality. And, of course, George recognized the value of an education.

So that was why George, even though he was perfectly happy at Iowa State, thought long and hard about Booker's offer. Tuskegee couldn't pay George as much money and didn't have the modern buildings or equipment. He would be leaving the comfort and security of one job for the uncertainty of another. But "the one great ideal of my life [is] to be of the greatest good to the greatest number of 'my people,'" George wrote to Booker. So he accepted the job, finished up his graduate degree at Iowa State, and arrived in Tuskegee in October 1896.

Chapter 6
Tuskegee

The city of Tuskegee and the surrounding area turned out to be an amazing place. George found many new plants and flowers to study. The school itself, however, wasn't so amazing. When George arrived, he had no rooms in which to store his collections, and not even a laboratory in which to work.

But George didn't worry about what he didn't have. "Use what you find around you," he told his first students. He took them to a junkyard. They dug up old pots and pans, saucers and spoons, boxes and string—

whatever they could find—and made their own laboratory.

It was all part of hands-on learning for George's students. He didn't want to just stand in front of a classroom and give lectures. He wanted his students to touch and feel nature—and to think.

On early morning walks, George collected samples of soil or flowers or insects that he shared in his classroom. Outside the classroom, he set up a practice farm on ten acres of land. It was an experiment station. One acre was for testing the soil, another was for growing sweet potatoes, another for studying fertilizers, and so on.

With the experiment station, George took his wish to be "the greatest good to the greatest number" seriously. He invited local farmers to come to the school once a month to learn about the soil.

During their monthly meetings, George analyzed the farmers' soil and gave them samples of his. Then he started encouraging them to come in between the monthly meetings,

whenever they needed some help. Then he invited the wives to come along, too. He showed them ways to plan meals and prepare food, and he discussed the value of different foods. George didn't have the money for fancy equipment at Tuskegee, so his advice was helpful to the farmers who didn't have the money for fancy equipment, either.

George wanted farmers to pay attention to nature and all it had to offer. He wrote different booklets that taught how to grow tomatoes or

raise hogs or preserve meat. The more farmers could do on their own, the less they had to spend at the market—and the less they had to go without. "Anything that fills the dinner pail is valuable," he said.

He wrote other booklets that helped farmers improve the appearance of their land and their homes. He knew they couldn't afford to buy paint, but he also knew there were plenty of natural resources. Different types of natural clay, for instance, could be mixed to make different colors for paint. With a little glue mixed in, it would stick to cabin walls. George also taught farmers how to care for native plants, flowers, and grasses, and how to fix up their homes.

Such a work schedule, though, was exhausting. George liked to get up by four o'clock in the morning and walk in the woods.

Then he taught four or five classes each day. He also ran the experiment station and worked in the homemade laboratory. He continued to paint and draw, too, and he often wrote letters to Moses and Susan Carver and to the other families he had lived with. He also organized a Bible study class once a week.

His intense workload and many interests left George little time for fun. Sometimes, his friends set him up on dates, but he never married.

In 1906, George designed the Jesup Agricultural Wagon.

It was a movable classroom and portable laboratory. The Jesup Wagon was named for a New York banker, Morris K. Jesup, who helped pay for it. A former student of George's was in charge of taking the wagon to faraway farmers who couldn't make it to Tuskegee. The wagon was loaded with soil, seeds, booklets, and other study materials.

In 1908, George had the chance to visit Moses, who had moved to Kansas after Susan's death several years earlier. It would be the last time George saw his foster father. Moses Carver died in his late nineties in 1910.

Five years after losing his father, George also lost his friend Booker T. Washington. Booker was fifty-nine when he died of heart failure in 1915. George and Booker didn't always agree on how things should be run at Tuskegee, but they were close friends. "I am sure Mr. Washington never knew how much I loved him, and the cause for which he gave his life," George wrote another friend.

Booker T. Washington had been the face of the Tuskegee Institute since the school opened its doors. After his death, Robert Russa Moton became president of Tuskegee. But it was George who became the most famous person at the school.

ROBERT RUSSA MOTON

Chapter 7
Peanuts!

While at Tuskegee, George liked to tell a story about a talk he had once had with God.

"Mr. Creator, why did you make the universe?" George asked.

"Little man, that question is too big for you," God answered. "Try another!"

So George asked, "Mr. Creator, why did you make man?"

God answered: "Little man, that question is still too big for you. Try another!"

This time George asked, "Mr. Creator, why did you make the peanut?"

And God said: "Little man, that question is just your size. You listen and I will teach you."

Apparently, George was a good listener, because

while experimenting at Tuskegee, he began to develop more than three hundred products that could be made from the peanut. They included everything from peanut milk to peanut punch, plastics, glue, soaps, and dyes.

Peanuts were considered so lowly that before George began to study them, they were mostly used for animal food. Farmers couldn't make much money from peanuts and had little reason to grow them.

Cotton had been the main crop in the American South. But in the early 1900s, it cost some farmers more to grow cotton than they could sell it for.

The boll weevil—a type
of beetle that feeds on
cotton buds and can
destroy entire crops—
came to the United States
from Mexico in the late 1800s.
By 1910, it had arrived in Alabama.

After many years of studying soil, George knew
that planting cotton over and over again sucked
the nutrients—substances plants need to grow—
out of the soil. He wanted farmers to rotate their
crops. That meant growing cotton one season, but
switching to a different crop the next. Then they
could replant cotton the season after that.

One of the crops
George recommended for
cotton growers was
the sweet potato.
Sweet potato plants
were easy to grow,

and crops could be stored during the winter months. They were good for the soil, and they could be eaten many different ways. Some of George's earliest bulletins were on the sweet potato. George also experimented with cowpeas, sugar beets, rice, soybeans, alfalfa, and more. His experiments helped him understand the best ways to grow these crops so that they would yield the most food. He learned what kinds of soil and growing conditions they needed.

In 1910, Tuskegee built George a modern laboratory to replace his homemade one. And by 1915, his experiments were taking so much of his time that he began to give up teaching.

In 1916, George wrote his most famous booklet: "How to Grow the Peanut, and 105 Ways of Preparing It for Human Consumption." Recipes included items such as peanut soup, peanut bread, and peanut pudding. Several recipes included peanut butter in them: Peanut butter was number fifty-one, peanut butter candy was number seventy, and peanut butter fudge was number eighty! In fact, George wrote so much about peanuts that he is sometimes mistakenly credited with inventing peanut butter.

The same year George produced his famous peanut booklet, he was honored by the Royal Society of Arts in London. The Royal Society honors people in science and art who find practical solutions to problems. That summed up

George perfectly! At the time, it was rare for an American to be honored—let alone one who had been born into slavery.

THE ROYAL SOCIETY OF ARTS

PEANUT BUTTER

MOST HISTORIANS BELIEVE PEANUT BUTTER HAS BEEN AROUND FOR HUNDREDS OF YEARS. BOTH THE INCA CIVILIZATION IN SOUTH AMERICA AND THE AZTECS OF ANCIENT MEXICO GROUND PEANUTS INTO PASTE.

IN THE UNITED STATES, DR. JOHN HENRY KELLOGG—FAMOUS FOR KELLOGG'S CEREALS—BELIEVED THAT PEANUT BUTTER WAS A VERY HEALTHY FOOD. HE MADE HIS OWN TYPE OF PEANUT BUTTER IN 1895. PEANUT BUTTER REALLY BECAME POPULAR AMONG THE AMERICAN PUBLIC AT THE ST. LOUIS WORLD'S FAIR IN 1904, ALONG WITH THE ICE-CREAM CONE AND COTTON CANDY.

Around this same time, George was reportedly offered a job to work for American inventor Thomas Edison in his New Jersey laboratory. George could have become rich working for Edison, but he was devoted to helping the farmers in the South. So he stayed at Tuskegee.

The *Peanut Journal* wrote that George Washington Carver "is to the peanut industry what [Thomas] Edison is to electricity." One biographer even called George "the patron saint" of the peanut industry.

THOMAS EDISON (1847–1931)

THOMAS ALVA EDISON WAS AN INVENTOR WHO CHANGED THE WORLD. HE INVENTED HUNDREDS OF ITEMS, INCLUDING SOME THAT HAD A GREAT INFLUENCE ON EVERYDAY LIFE, SUCH AS THE FIRST PRACTICAL LIGHTBULB, THE PHONOGRAPH, AND THE MOTION-PICTURE CAMERA.

EDISON WAS KNOWN FOR WORKING TIRELESSLY AT HIS LABORATORIES IN MENLO PARK, NEW JERSEY. (HIS NICKNAME WAS "THE WIZARD OF MENLO PARK.") HE FAMOUSLY SAID, "GENIUS IS ONE PERCENT INSPIRATION AND NINETY-NINE PERCENT PERSPIRATION."

Chapter 8
Lasting Impact

George was never interested in personal glory, but his work with peanuts made him famous. In 1921, he took a train to Washington, DC, to talk to Congress about the peanut industry.

George was supposed to give a ten-minute talk. But when his ten minutes were up, the politicians gave him another ten minutes. And when those ten minutes were up, they told him to talk for as long as he needed! George pulled samples out of a box to show different ways peanuts could be used: in milk, breakfast foods, oils, and more. Texas congressman John N. Garner, who later became vice president of the United States, called it "a most wonderful exhibition." Congress passed a law that helped the peanut industry. After that, George wrote newspaper and magazine articles about the peanut industry, and he advised companies that produced peanuts.

He also continued working at Tuskegee. He no longer taught classes, but focused on his work in the laboratory instead. He came to be known as a "creative chemist"—a scientist who remakes a product, such as peanuts in George's case, for different uses. He received awards from organizations such as the National Association for the Advancement of Colored People (NAACP). He also began working with the United States Department

of Agriculture to help identify and prevent plant diseases in the South.

Though he discovered hundreds of nonfood uses for the peanut, and many for the sweet potato, too, none of George's products were sold to the public. George's goal was never to get rich, though.

He rarely spent the money he did make, unless it was to help a former student who needed a loan. He was known for wearing the same old clothes day after day.

Even after he began receiving awards and honors for his work, George wanted to find ways to help people. He still taught his weekly Bible study class, and he always was willing to help any student in need. He was like a second father to many of them and offered sound words of advice.

THE WISDOM OF
GEORGE WASHINGTON CARVER

"HOW FAR YOU GO IN LIFE DEPENDS ON YOUR BEING TENDER WITH THE YOUNG, COMPASSIONATE WITH THE AGED, SYMPATHETIC WITH THE STRIVING, AND TOLERANT OF THE WEAK AND STRONG. BECAUSE SOMEDAY IN YOUR LIFE YOU WILL HAVE BEEN ALL OF THESE."

"WHEN YOU CAN DO THE COMMON THINGS OF LIFE IN AN UNCOMMON WAY, YOU WILL COMMAND THE ATTENTION OF THE WORLD."

"START WHERE YOU ARE WITH WHAT YOU HAVE. MAKE SOMETHING OF IT AND NEVER BE SATISFIED."

"EDUCATION IS THE KEY TO UNLOCK THE GOLDEN DOOR OF FREEDOM."

"READING ABOUT NATURE IS FINE, BUT IF A PERSON WALKS IN THE WOODS AND LISTENS CAREFULLY, HE CAN LEARN MORE THAN WHAT IS IN BOOKS."

"NINETY-NINE PERCENT OF THE FAILURES COME FROM PEOPLE WHO HAVE THE HABIT OF MAKING EXCUSES."

In 1937, to celebrate George's forty years at the Tuskegee Institute, the school unveiled a bronze bust of him on campus. A press release and notices in the *Peanut Journal* asked for $1 donations to pay for the artwork. People—both black and white—who admired George sent in their donations from all over the country.

Two years later, the George Washington Carver Museum opened in Tuskegee. It included parts of

George's original homemade laboratory, samples
of the peanut products he created, educational

exhibits, and much more. Dozens of George's paintings hung on the walls. In 1940, George donated his entire life savings—about $60,000—to start the George Washington Carver Foundation at the Tuskegee Institute for agricultural research. He wanted others to continue his work at Tuskegee even after he was gone.

In his later years, George's health began to fail him, but he didn't stop working. In December 1942, he hurt himself when he fell down some stairs at the museum. He never fully recovered, and he died in January 1943. It is believed he

was seventy-eight years old. He was buried next to his friend Booker T. Washington on the Tuskegee campus.

Five years after George's death, he became only the second black American to be depicted on a postage stamp. Booker T. Washington had been the first. In 1953, in Diamond Grove, Missouri, he became the first black American to have a national monument dedicated to him. Hundreds of schools across the United States are now named for this great scientist.

Critics say that most of George's work did not produce amazing breakthroughs or discoveries. Instead, he found practical ways for science to make people's lives better.

In many ways, George was ahead of his time. He understood the importance of nutrition and a balanced diet long before many others did. He saw value in caring for the environment and growing fruits and vegetables naturally.

GEORGE WASHINGTON CARVER

He recycled items that had been discarded and found new uses for them. George helped the economy in the American South.

He helped farmers move away from their dependency on growing cotton. And he helped poor farmers find ways to take care of themselves. He did all that while never losing the passion for nature that he first showed in his youth.

As George's tombstone at Tuskegee reads: "He could have added fortune to fame, but caring for neither, he found happiness and honor in being helpful to the world."

TIMELINE OF GEORGE WASHINGTON CARVER'S LIFE

c. 1864 — George is born in Diamond Grove, Missouri

1877 — Begins formal schooling in Neosho, Missouri

1885 — Is accepted to Highland College, but is denied admission when administrators there see that he is black

1886 — Works as a homesteader in Ness County, Kansas, and begins performing agricultural experiments on the farm

1894 — Graduates from Iowa State and joins the faculty there

1896 — Earns a master's degree in agriculture from Iowa State and joins famed educator Booker T. Washington on the staff of Tuskegee Institute in Alabama

1906 — Designs the Jesup Wagon for practical demonstrations to farmers

1916 — Produces his bulletin "How to Grow the Peanut, and 105 Ways of Preparing It for Human Consumption" Named a fellow for the London Royal Society for the Encouragement of the Arts

1921 — Speaks to the US Congress House Ways and Means Committee about uses for the peanut

1923 — Is awarded the NAACP's Spingarn Medal for distinguished service to science

1928 — Receives an honorary doctor of science degree from Simpson College

1935 — Begins working with the US Department of Agriculture on the study of plant diseases

1940 — Establishes the George Washington Carver Research Foundation at Tuskegee

1943 — Dies on January 5 in Tuskegee, Alabama

TIMELINE OF THE WORLD

Abraham Lincoln is elected the sixteenth president of the United States — **1860**

The American Civil War begins — **1861**

President Lincoln issues the Emancipation Proclamation — **1863**

The American Civil War ends
President Lincoln is assassinated — **1865**

Thomas Edison invents the first commercially practical incandescent lightbulb — **1879**

Ellis Island opens — **1892**

German physicist Wilhelm Röntgen discovers X-rays — **1895**

The Supreme Court's *Plessy v. Ferguson* decision establishes the segregation doctrine of "separate but equal" — **1896**

The Wright brothers fly a plane at Kitty Hawk, North Carolina — **1903**

The ocean liner *Titanic* sinks on its first voyage — **1912**

World War I begins in Europe — **1914**

World War I ends — **1918**

A major flu epidemic, which began in 1918, kills between 30 and 50 million people around the world — **1919**

The Nineteenth Amendment gives women the right to vote in the United States — **1920**

The New York stock market crashes — **1929**

Franklin Delano Roosevelt is elected president of the United States for the first of a record four terms — **1932**

The United States officially enters World War II after Japan attacks Pearl Harbor in Hawaii — **1941**

BIBLIOGRAPHY

* Bolden, Tonya. **George Washington Carver**. New York: Abrams Books for Young Readers, 2008.

* Collins, David. **George Washington Carver: Man's Slave Becomes God's Scientist**. Fenton, MI: Mott Media, 2005.

* Harness, Cheryl. **The Groundbreaking, Chance-Taking Life of George Washington Carver and Science and Invention in America**. Washington, DC: National Geographic Children's Books, 2008.

* Labrecque, Ellen. **George Washington Carver (Science Biographies)**. Chicago: Raintree, 2014.

* Books for young readers

* MacLeod, Elizabeth. **George Washington Carver: An Innovative Life**. Toronto: Kids Can Press, 2007.

McMurry, Linda O. **George Washington Carver: Scientist & Symbol**. New York: Oxford University Press, 1981.

* Moore, Eva. **The Story of George Washington Carver**. New York: Scholastic, 1990.

Wellman, Sam. **George Washington Carver**. North Newton, KS: Wild Centuries Press, 2013.

THE TIME-TRAVELING ADVENTURES OF THE ROBBINS TWINS

THE TREASURE CHEST

"Kids who have outgrown the
'Magic Treehouse' may enjoy this new series."
—*School Library Journal*

Join Felix and Maisie Robbins on their trips through time as they
meet thrilling historical figures as children in *New York Times*
Best-Selling author Ann Hood's *The Treasure Chest*!